HORIZONTAL PARENTING

HORIZONTAL PARENTING

How to Entertain Your Kid While Lying Down

MICHELLE WOO

ILLUSTRATED BY DASHA TOLSTIKOVA

CHRONICLE BOOKS
SAN FRANCISCO

Library of Congress Cataloging-in-Publication Data

Names: Woo, Michelle (Writer and editor), author. | Tolstikova, Dasha, illustrator.
Title: Horizontal parenting : how to entertain your kid while lying down / Michelle Woo ; illustrated by Dasha Tolstikova.
Description: San Francisco : Chronicle Books, [2021]
Identifiers: LCCN 2021007699 |
ISBN 9781797211343 (hardcover)
Subjects: LCSH: Parent and child--Humor. |
Parenting--Humor. | Games.
Classification: LCC PN6231.P2 W66 2021 | DDC 790.1--dc23
LC record available at https://lccn.loc.gov/2021007699

Manufactured in India.

MIX
Paper from responsible sources
FSC www.fsc.org   FSC™ C016779

Design by Rachel Harrell.

Illustrations by Dasha Tolstikova.

The information contained in this book is presented for educational (and entertainment) purposes only. Use common sense and don't actually fall asleep (or let your kid put a cactus on your butt) while parenting.

10 9 8 7 6 5 4 3 2

Bubble Wrap is a registered trademark of Sealed Air Corporation. Etch A Sketch is a registered trademark of Spin Master Ltd. *The Great British Baking Show* is a registered trademark of Love Productions Limited. *Law & Order* is a registered trademark of NBCUniversal Media, LLC. Operation is a registered trademark of Hasbro, Inc. PAW Patrol is a registered trademark of Spin Master Ltd. Riverdance is a registered trademark of Riverdance Limited, LLC.

Chronicle books and gifts are available at special quantity discounts to corporations, professional associations, literacy programs, and other organizations. For details and discount information, please contact our premiums department at corporatesales@chroniclebooks.com or at 1-800-759-0190.

Chronicle Books LLC
680 Second Street
San Francisco, California 94107
www.chroniclebooks.com

For Maggie and Max: You make me so tired, but so happy. —M. W.

For my parent friends, some of whom are in this book. —D. T.

Contents

INTRODUCTION

"Just rest," I would tell my daughter, Maggie, pretty much the moment she learned how to walk. As a young kid, she'd zip around the house like a distracted squirrel, asking me to play with her here, then over there, then back over here again.

"Let's look at the fish tank!" she'd say, motioning me toward her. "Wanna hop like bunnies? Catch the ball, Mama!"

Yearning to park my exhausted body in one place, I'd call out to her defeatedly: "How about we . . . just rest?"

When you become a parent, you learn that the energy level of children is woefully disproportionate to the energy level of adults. You try to keep up, but there are times when you just can't—maybe you had a long day at work, or you're not feeling well, or you are forty.

Fortunately, there is relief. I've discovered a secret that savvy moms and dads have known for ages, one that allows you to relax on demand. Listen closely, weary parents of the world: It's time to start entertaining your kids *while lying down.*

What you're about to learn is called horizontal parenting, and all it requires are some basic household items and your imagination. Have a washable marker? Let your child make "mole constellations," connecting the sunspots on your back. Got some painter's tape? Great. Your kid is now a CSI agent who must create an outline of the victim's body (read: yours). See some blankets? Excellent. You're a burrito ready to be rolled by a tiny burrito maker. The idea here is to use your listless body as an activity source. Make up ridiculous stories. Lean into the weird.

In this guide, you'll find fifty games and activities that you can do with your kids while collapsed on the sofa or floor. Refer to this book often—maybe even tonight when you're counting down the minutes to that glorious hour known as "bedtime."

And don't worry if anyone walks past your sprawled-out body, wondering why your child is drawing the Big Dipper in your armpit. Simply smile, give them a look of assurance, and say, "Hey, we're playing here."

"You're nineteen
carrots tall, Mama."

"Nice! Try peas next."

How Tall Am I?

Grown-ups are tall. But how tall? Have your kid estimate your height in whatever household objects you have on hand: cereal boxes, cans of soup, sneakers, sheets of toilet paper, docile pets. Then tell them to line up the items next to your body and count them. Were they close? No? Try again with something even smaller this time.

BONUS POINTS:
Use tiny crackers and a clean floor and this one doubles as snack time.

A Portrait of Rest

So your kid is a budding Michelangelo—or at least that's what Grandma tells her knitting club pals. Have them draw a portrait of you while you nap. If you have multiple kids, you can even turn it into an art contest. Remind them that details are important, especially the dark circles underneath your eyes caused by years of sleep deprivation.

BONUS POINTS:
Have your kid use an Etch A Sketch.

"Don't forget to color
in Dad's drool."

Hide-and-Seek-ish

The next time your kid begs, "Can you play hide-and-seek with me, pleeeeeease?" introduce them to this new and highly improved version of the game. How it works: As you count to twenty, your kid hides. When you finish counting, instead of embarking on a search through your home, just shout out your guesses from your comfy resting spot: "Are you underneath the bathroom sink?" "Behind the living room planter?" "Gosh, this is tricky. I bet you're in the pantry!" When you guess correctly, your kid must emerge from their hiding spot and the game starts again.

BONUS POINTS:
Use a baby monitor intercom
as a microphone.

Crime Scene

Calling all amateur detectives and *Law & Order* extras: There's been an incident at 100 Living Room Lane, where a body has been found sprawled out on the floor. Yours. Presumed cause of death: listening to "The Wheels on the Bus" on full volume 7,592 times. Your kid is a CSI agent and their mission is to get to the bottom of the case. Using a roll of painter's tape, ask them to make an outline of your body to submit as evidence.

BONUS POINTS:
Have your kid take fingerprints of every one of your fingers and toeprints of every one of your toes.

Ninja Walk

A tiny stealth ninja has invaded your home. This one is swift, silent, and, come to think of it, looks a lot like your kid. As you lie facedown on the floor and close your eyes, have them walk past you as quietly as possible. If you hear the slightest sound, yell, "Ninja!" and send them back to the starting line. Again.

BONUS POINTS:
Roll up a small T-shirt or towel to make "nunchucks" and try to throw one end at your kid as they walk by.

Doogie Howser Junior

Your kid just graduated from a questionable medical school and guess what? You're their first test patient. Create a life-size version of the game Operation by placing various small items all over your body. Using a pair of kitchen tongs, your kid must surgically remove the items and place them onto a tray, no hands allowed. If the tongs touch your body or if any of the items fall to the ground, make a loud buzzing sound, start convulsing wildly, and reset the game.

BONUS POINTS:
After a successful surgery, let your kid bandage you up with stickers.

Sleeping Beauty

When you can barely keep your eyes open, announce that you will be acting out a scene from the classic fairy tale *Sleeping Beauty*. You'll play the title character, of course. Have your kid gather as many stuffed animals as they can find and arrange them in a line leading up to your snoozing body. One by one, each stuffie must give you a kiss to find out if they're your true love. Lambchops: "Smooch!" Scruffy Bear: "Muah!" Have this go on for a while. Wait, how does this story end? Who knows? The important thing is that you lived restfully ever after.

Roll the Burrito

When breakfast was at 5:30 a.m. and lunch is still hours away . . . it's burrito time. Lie down on a blanket, pretending it's a giant tortilla. Let your kid pile on the "ingredients." Have some rolls of dress socks? Those can be the meat or beans. Thirty different Elmo stuffies lying around? Hello, salsa. Top with pillow sour cream and make sure to narrate the whole process. "Here comes the guacamole! That'll cost extra!" The grand finale is rolling you up.

BONUS POINTS:
Make up a burrito song to the tune of
"Peanut, Peanut Butter and Jelly."

"A little cilantro will
round out the flavor!"

Railroad to Relaxation

All aboard, friends! This is one train you shouldn't miss. Lie facedown. Have your kid roll their toy trains around your back and up and down your legs. They get Grand Central Station, while you get something that almost feels like a massage.

BONUS POINTS:
Grab an old white T-shirt and have your kid draw tracks on the back that the trains can follow.

Belly Bass Drum

Who needs expensive music classes when your kid has the best instrument right here? That's right—your belly. Whether you have a six-pack or some extra padding, lie down and let your stomach double as a drum. Then simply close your eyes and let yourself be swept away by the new samba hit "Oh God, I Shouldn't Have Had Those Two Roast Beef Sandwiches Five Minutes Ago."

BONUS POINTS:
Add a cowbell. More cowbell.

The Night Before Christmas

It's Christmas Eve and you're snug in your bed, ready for visions of sugarplums and post-holiday online sales to dance in your head. (Don't worry if it's actually hot and humid in mid-July—young children have a frail grasp of time.) Give your little Santa some old newspaper and tape, and have them wrap up various items around the house to bring to you as gifts while you sleep. "Wake up" on Christmas morning, open your gifts, and thank Santa, who's already back at the North Pole (or maybe behind the sofa, giggling).

BONUS POINTS:
Any gifting holiday works. Individually wrapped puzzle pieces make a wonderful birthday gift.

Don't Wake the Giant

You are a giant sleeping on the sofa, chair, or floor, just minding your own giant business. As your kids (and maybe a few of their friends) run around you in circles, "wake up" at random to catch the trespassers. Suddenly, you win the title of best playdate chaperone ever.

BONUS POINTS:
To add to the excitement, throw in some giant snores and moments when you almost wake up but fall back asleep.

What's on My Butt?

[*Game show announcer's voice*] "It's time to play every tired parent's favorite game . . . What's on My Butt?" While lying facedown, have your kid place a household item on your bottom and try to guess what it is. Wiggle your cheeks around to get a better feel. The most important part of the game is to say the word *butt* in your most dramatic voice. "Is there a picture frame . . . on my *butt*?" "A loaf of bread . . . on my *butt*?" "A ukulele . . . on my *butt*?"

Amnesia

Oh dear. You've somehow bumped your head and are experiencing severe memory loss. As you lie in bed, your kid must help you piece together what happened by bringing you various "clues" from around the house. "I remember holding a tube of toothpaste." [*Kid runs to grab a tube of toothpaste.*] "Oh yes! And for some reason, I recall reaching for a spatula." [*They find a spatula.*] After seeing the many clues, let it all come together to form a wild story. Whew, all that remembering took a lot of energy. It's time for a nap.

"There was definitely some cheese involved . . . and crackers. I'm having visions of crackers."

Tiny Tooth Fairy

Your kid is the tooth fairy and you've just lost a tooth. As you sleep, they must place coins, small gifts, and notes underneath your pillow, and then run and hide. When you "wake up" and check to see what the tooth fairy brought, you suddenly feel something wiggling in your mouth. What's this? Oh boy, you've just lost another tooth! Time to go back to sleep. (Note: This is better done after your kid is hip to the tooth fairy operation. Or else you risk stealing all sense of magic and wonder in the world, that's all.)

BONUS POINTS:
Try using candy corn as teeth!

Car Wash

No time for a shower this morning? Throw on a bathing suit, get horizontal in the tub, and pretend you're a car at the car wash. Have your kid mark up your body with washable finger paint, globs of body scrub, and expired mud mask residue. Then have them clean you off using rags, soap, and a bucket of water. Don't forget to tip!

BONUS POINTS:
For extra shine, opt for a body butter "wax" as an add-on.

Lazy Yoga

Cue the tranquil music. Welcome to a special nonjudgmental Parent and Me yoga session. Our intention for today is to focus on poses that don't require lifting our bodies off the floor. Try Child's Pose (have your kid lie facedown on your back), Bow Pose (let them hang on your shoulders), and the tired parent's favorite: Savasana, a.k.a. Corpse Pose (hug their body as you lie on the ground). Stay there until bedtime.

BONUS POINTS:
Everyone knows it counts as a workout if you wear yoga pants.

Couch Potato

Ahhhh, it's time to kick up your feet and watch some TV. Hey, would you look at that? It's your kid on the screen! You have a magical remote control that makes them act out whatever show you choose. So, what will you watch today? A wildlife documentary, the World Cup, or *The Great British Baking Show*, perhaps? Or best of all—a silent film?

"Make sure to get
my elbows. They're
a little dry."

Lotion Painting

It's finally time to make use of that bottle of Razzle Raspberry body lotion that Aunt Rita gave you for your birthday in 2001. Pour some into a small cup, stick a paintbrush inside, and declare it painting time. Today's canvas: you.

Service with a Smile

You've just booked a room at the newest five-star hotel in town: Chateau de Toddler. (The online reviews were terrible, but the rate was only seven graham crackers, so you're going with it.) When you arrive, you're greeted by a small butler: your child. They're here to provide whatever you need, whether it's a fluffed pillow, a lullaby, or three gummy worms served on a tray. All you need to say is "Room service!"

BONUS POINTS:
If you have a bell, ring it with abandon.

Cave Explorer

Your kid is a spelunker. With a headlamp or flashlight, have them crawl through a dark room and brave underground dangers like bats and cobwebs, which could be dangling toilet paper or streamers. Their goal is to uncover the fossil of a long-forgotten species, Exhausted Parentosaurus, which is believed to have gone extinct after hearing the words "Not the blue cup! I want the green cup!" one too many times.

BONUS POINTS:
After they finish exploring every dark corner of the cave, have them draw a detailed map of the terrain they discovered.

Construction Site Night-Night

Twenty minutes until bedtime and out of ideas? *Beep beep.* Your kid is a construction worker and you're their excavator. Lie on your stomach, rest your eyes, and have your kid sit on you, facing your feet. Bend your knees so your feet are in the air. Your legs are now the throttle control levers. Time to dig as you count the final minutes until you can back this mighty truck into a kid-free bubble bath.

"Look, I caught a 'What Happens in Vegas' magnet!"

Couch Fishing

It's a beautiful day to go fishing . . . on your couch. First, you'll need a fishing pole. Find any stick in your home—a ruler, a toy golf club, that old drumstick you used back when you were in a band and stayed out past 9 p.m. Attach a string to it and tie a magnet to the end of the string. For your "fish," grab some magnets off the refrigerator and sprinkle them on the floor next to your couch. Then hop onto your couch-boat with your kid and see what you catch.

BONUS POINTS:
Use gummy worms for "bait."

Packing Peanut Angels

Making snow angels is a classic childhood tradition, but if there's none of that fluffy white stuff where you live, you'll have to improvise. Gather lots of small objects from around your home and lie down. You can make packing peanut angels, or craft-bead angels, or even dried bean angels! Just sweep your arms and legs up and down for the next twenty minutes, or until one of you gets tired.

BONUS POINTS:
Stick dusting cloths under your limbs.
Now you're cleaning your floors too.

"Waaaaaaah!"

"What do you need?
A bottle? A diaper
change? The *New York
Times* crossword?"

Meet the New Baby

There's a brand-new baby in the house: you. You're the baby and your kid is the exasperated parent who has to feed you, burp you, change you, sing to you, and google things at 3 a.m. like "newborn poop color chart" and "Will I ever get to sleep again?"

Mousetrap

Oh no, you've got a mouse problem. Only this infestation will last until they pack up for college. Still, you might as well try to trap 'em. Lie on your back and lift one leg up. As your kids crawl around you in circles, gently snap your legs together at random to see if you can catch them one at a time.

Animal Parade

So your house has become a zoo. Just embrace it and welcome the animal parade. Lie on the floor, close your eyes, and listen as your kid walks past you in different ways—stomping like an elephant, tiptoeing like a cat, hopping on one foot like a flamingo, crawling like a crab. See if you can guess which animal is passing by.

Dream Charades

You have fallen into a deep sleep on the couch. With your eyes closed, act out a scene and have your kid guess what's happening in Dreamland. Are you competing in a hot dog eating contest? Being chased by hungry alligators? Auditioning for *Riverdance*? If they guess correctly, make a loud snoring sound and move on to the next dream.

Change of Scenery

If you feel like the days of the week are blending together, 1. Welcome to parenthood, and 2. You could probably use a change of scenery. Grab a long piece of butcher paper or a giant piece of cardboard and lie down on it. Have your kid draw a scene featuring you as the star. What will you become? An astronaut? A late-night show host? A collector of stray cats?

BONUS POINTS:
Let your kid direct you in a movie scene that you act out while lying on your new backdrop.

Carpet Camping

Who says camping has to involve bug bites, achy backs, and a constant fear of running out of toilet paper? When carpet camping, simply lay out some sleeping bags in your living room and pretend you're roughing it in the woods. You can tell ghost stories, sing campfire songs, and stick a flashlight under a colander to gaze at the "stars." Remind your kids to keep their voices to a whisper—they don't want to wake the bears.

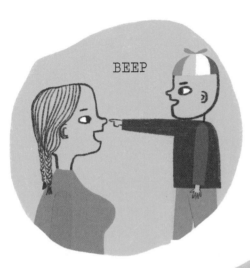

BEEP

BOOP

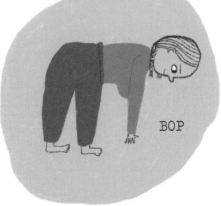

BOP

Fix the Robot

System error! You are a robot that has malfunctioned. Your kid must try to fix you by pressing different combinations of buttons on your body: "nose-nose-chin-knee," "elbow-ear-head-head," "pinkie-eyebrow-shoulder-belly." Make *beep-bop-boop* noises and twitch your limbs every once in a while to show that their efforts are working.

BONUS POINTS:
Let them give you a robot makeover by wrapping your limbs in aluminum foil and placing a paper bag over your head.

Extra Postage Required

"Excuse me, young mail worker, but this package needs extra-special handling." Have your kid gather up all the "packing supplies" they can find to help keep you safe on your very long journey to No Whiningville, Alaska. Blankets can be Bubble Wrap. Stickers can be stamps. Let them know that any returns will take seven to ten business days—or as long as needed to get in a good nap.

M Is for Massage

Save the trees by having your kid write letters or words with their finger on your back. Try to guess what they're spelling.

BONUS POINTS:
Grab a dictionary and ask your kid to write out the longest word they can find.

Held Captive

You're a dungeon master who's lying down on a comfy dungeon sofa. Perched along your body are your captives (a.k.a. your kids' stuffed animals). As you sleep, your kids must rescue the cuddly prisoners without waking you up. One wrong move and they might face the same fate as Bear Bear and Mrs. Fluffy Muffin.

Day Spa

Ooh la la, it's spa day. Let your kid pamper you from head to toe, resting warm towels on your forehead, plopping cool cucumber slices on your eyes, massaging your hands with scented oil, and topping it all off with a full pedicure. Your feet might end up looking like Jackson Pollock paintings, but at least you'll get ten minutes of peace.

Snail Trails

How slow can you go? You and your kid are snails slithering on the floor. Your goal is to get to the other side of the house, but in this game, the *last* one wins.

"Oh no, Fluff
is winning!"

Catch the Firefly

Re-create the magic of chasing fireflies on a warm summer night. Turn off the lights and turn on a flashlight. The light is the firefly. Have your kid try to "catch" it as you move it around the room, stopping it at random. "Look, it's above your head!" "Now it's on the floor." Watch as they reach for it, stomp on it, and chase it with glee—all while you stay put.

BONUS POINTS:
The game works for cats too.

Tattoo Parlor

You're about to get the most epic, badass tattoo when you discover that the artist is none other than . . . your kid. Wonderful. Now your design choices are limited to a happy face, a sun, or something that might either be a slice of toast or Uncle Marty's face—it's unclear. Oh well. At least their inking tool of choice is a washable marker. Roll up your sleeve and let them get to work.

BONUS POINTS:
Mix in some temporary tattoos for a full-sleeve effect. You can never have enough unicorn ink.

Dead Fish

In the game of Dead Fish, you are a fish that may or may not be dead. Your kid observes you very, very closely and if they detect any movement—an eye twitch, a nose wriggle, the curling of your pinkie toe—they must yell, "FISH NOT DEAD! FISH NOT DEAD!" and toss you back into the bowl to swim another day.

BONUS POINTS:
On hot days, hand your kid a spray bottle of water and let them spritz you, the possibly dead fish, if they detect any sign of life.

Hibernation Mode

You and your kid are groundhogs getting ready to hibernate during the long, cold winter. Your job is to guard the burrow (a.k.a. your favorite spot on the sofa) while your little groundhog gathers the food: leaves, berries, insects, and *maybe* some of those cookies you tucked away in the pantry. Once you have everything you need, snuggle up together and prepare to enter a dormant state for the next several months—OK, fine, you'll take seven minutes.

"Set my alarm
for next spring."

Comforter Cocoon

You've stumbled upon a magical metamorphosing cocoon, which happens to be in the form of a cozy sleeping bag or blanket. Lie down and wrap yourself in it. Tell your kid to be *very* patient as you transform into something new. They may ask you questions about what you're becoming: "Do you have fur?" "Can you fly?" "Are you a character from *PAW Patrol*?" Make some noises and gestures to let them know if they're on the right track. After a few guesses, emerge from the blanket and reveal what you are. Then go back into your cocoon and transform into something else.

I Lava You

If parenthood won't allow you to take the relaxing Hawaiian vacation you've been daydreaming about, bring the island home by pretending to be a volcano. Lie on your back and have your kid pile blankets and pillows on top of you. But tell them to be careful because this volcano is active. "Erupt" at random times by throwing the blankets and pillows everywhere, and watch as your kid flees the room in terror and delight.

Mole Constellations

Need an activity that's part astronomy lesson, part prep for your next dermatologist appointment? Hand your kid a washable marker and let them connect your moles, sunspots, scars, and freckles to make weird and beautiful constellations.

BONUS POINTS:
To draw this one out another ten minutes, tell your kid it's time to stare at the constellations in silent awe. You're "stargazing."

Will It Roll?

Give your kid a lesson in physics while giving yourself a nap. Grab a stack of pillows—five to seven is ideal—and lie on them, facedown, so your back becomes a ramp. Now let your kid find out what rolls by testing various objects in your home: markers, a bottle of shampoo, a baseball, a paper towel tube, Mr. Whiskers. See if their hypotheses were correct.

"Meow!"

"Ziggy, it looks like we've got an avalanche!"

Rescue Me

Help! You're stuck under a pile of debris—pillows, cushions, and blankets. Luckily, your child has transformed into—dun-dun-dun-dun—Super Rescue Kid! This little hero is ready to save the day. Just call them on the Super Rescue Kid phone line and tell them your location. When they pull you out to safety, thank them and tell them another thing real heroes do: put all the cushions back where they belong.

The Claw

If you've ever wanted to play the claw arcade game without spending $22 in quarters and walking away with an armful of nothing, here's how to make your own for free: Lie facedown on the sofa and place a pile of stuffed animals on the floor next to you, within your reach. Create a "claw," with a pair of large tongs, a reacher aid, or your hand. Have your kid direct the claw to the perfect position—"A little to the left!" "Move back!" "Right there!" When they say, "Drop," drop the claw, close it, and see if you grabbed anything.

What's Different?

How perceptive are you, really? Scan your surroundings and close your eyes.

With your eyes closed, have your kid rearrange a few items within your view.

When you open your eyes, try to figure out what's different.

BONUS POINTS:

Really take your time, making some probably incorrect guesses, such as, "That crumpled receipt on the table is half a millimeter to the left, isn't it?"

The Horizontal Hokey Pokey

"You put your right foot in, you put your right foot out." Ah, the "Hokey Pokey": a song loved by young children, and bad wedding DJs. Do the moves with your kid while lying down. When it's time to "turn yourself around," roll around on the floor. That's what it's all about.

BONUS POINTS:
Now try the "Horizontal Macarena."

Secret Agents

Tell your kid to do something and they'll look at you with suspicion. But tell them they're a spy with a "secret mission" and watch them giddily follow your commands. As the spy boss (that's you), lounge around while giving them a series of tasks: "Count the windows in the house," "Do twelve jumping jacks," or "Spell out a word using the letters in the ingredient list on the cereal box." After they complete the whole list, say "Mission Complete."

The Nap Game

At last, it's the horizontal parenting classic, an activity passed down from generation to generation. In the Nap Game, there's only one rule: Whoever can stay quiet the longest wins. Play it anywhere and everywhere. Play it often and without shame. Hey, why not even play it right now? Grab a pillow and make yourself comfortable. Then, as you look back at your former parenting life, the one that involved standing, moving, and sitting down only to just get back up, close your eyes and smile. You've come so far, you brilliant parent, you.

(Actually, uh, you haven't moved in three hours. Maybe it's time to fix your kid some breakfast?)

"I love this game."

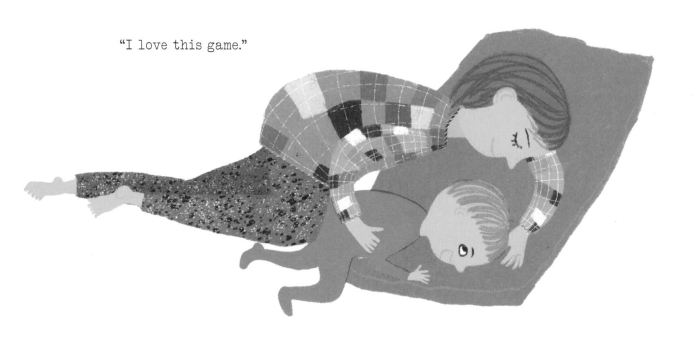

About the Author

Michelle Woo is an award-winning journalist. She was the parenting editor at *Lifehacker*, where she wrote about tricks and strategies to make life as a parent easier and even fun. She is a senior editor at Medium. Her work has appeared on CNN, *Jezebel*, *Gizmodo*, *Narratively*, and in *USA Today*. She lives in Southern California with her husband, Matt, and her kids, Maggie and Max.

About the Illustrator

Dasha Tolstikova is an award-winning author and illustrator. Her work has appeared in the *Wall Street Journal*, the *New York Times*, and the *New Yorker*, among others. Her book *A Year Without Mom* garnered four starred reviews and was named a *Kirkus* Best Middle-Grade Book of the Year. Dasha has been practicing horizontal parenting since 2003, challenging her then two-year-old baby sister to "see who can keep their eyes closed longer" whenever she came to wake Dasha up at 5:00 a.m. Dasha lives in New York City with her dog, Muffin. Find out more about her latest book, *The Bad Chair* (a tale of subterfuge and friendship), at www.dashatolstikova.com.